Peter's Pictures

by
Lyn Wendon

Illustrations by Jane Launchbury
Colourist: Amanda Hall

Collins Educational
An imprint of HarperCollinsPublishers

This picture will have lots and lots of dots on it, and lots and lots of spots.

Sit on this bit of paper. Good puppy.
Stand on that bit. Good puppy.
Wag your tail. Good puppy.